D0647018

CHICKEN
Parade

"Be bold and boastful, just like the cock beside the hen." —Aeschylus

CHICKEN
Parade

METRO BOOKS
New York

For centuries they awoke humans with their song, punctually announcing the rising sun, before their "cock-a-doodle-doo" was replaced by the no less insistent ringing of alarm clocks. Proud, full of ardor, and often quarrelsome, roosters are the undisputed sovereigns of a kingdom of feathers, bona fide star performers and seasoned actors on the stage of the chicken run. They roam about with their severe air of control and measured step, dominating their territory and subjects, and shaking their crimson wattles and crests with studied theatrics. The hens, their life companions, placid and indifferent, appear not to pay much attention to such masculine display. They have other things to think about: minding the clutches of peeping chicks that run about in all directions, or remaining motionless, attentively brooding their eggs. The roosters never cease sounding their continual "cock-a-doodle-doo." A constant chatter supplying the soundtrack for a day in the life of a fowl. A world in miniature, that of the chicken coop; but is it so remote, so different from the human world?

"DON'T COUNT YOUR CHICKENS BEFORE THEY HATCH."

–Aesop

"Are you talking to me?"

~Robert De Niro, *Taxi Driver*

CHALLENGE
TO THE LAST FEATHER

"Morning comes whether you set the alarm or not."

–Ursula K. LeGuin

THE FABULOUS 1970s

"The cock, that is the trumpet to the morn."

−Alexander Hamilton

15

DOMESTIC QUARRELS

"Surrounding yourself with dwarfs
does not make you a giant."

–Yiddish Proverb

Once
upon a
t i m e
there was an extraordinary hen that laid a golden
egg every day. Because of his greediness, the farmer
after some time was no longer satisfied with the single egg that the hen regularly laid for him: "I bet if I
killed it, I would become rich. Who knows how much
gold it has in its belly? Useless to stand around wait-
ing for just one miserable egg every day!" he
thought confidently. But he ended up realizing that
the amazing chicken was, in fact, no different
than other chickens, and had no gold inside
her, as he had foolishly imagined. So, because he could not be content with what
he had, he remained without anything
since now he could no longer
even count on the single
egg   each   day.

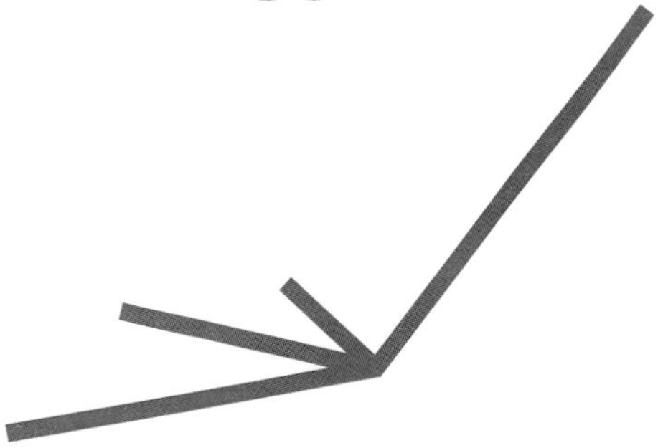

"A secret is not something
unrevealed,
but something told
privately, in a whisper."

–Marcel Pagnol

EVOLUTIONARY PATH

PUNK

"Those who stand for nothing, fall for anything."

~Alexander Hamilton

THE HUNTER

"Having one son makes you a parent; having two makes you a referee."

–David Frost

AT THE BAR

37

"I'M LATE. I'M LATE!"

–White Rabbit

SIDE A

THE DUELISTS

–Ridley Scott

"The cocks may crow, but it's the hen that lays the egg."

~Margaret Thatcher

FORWARD, MARCH!

CALCULATING THE RISK

FAST FOOD

DIFFICULT APPROACH

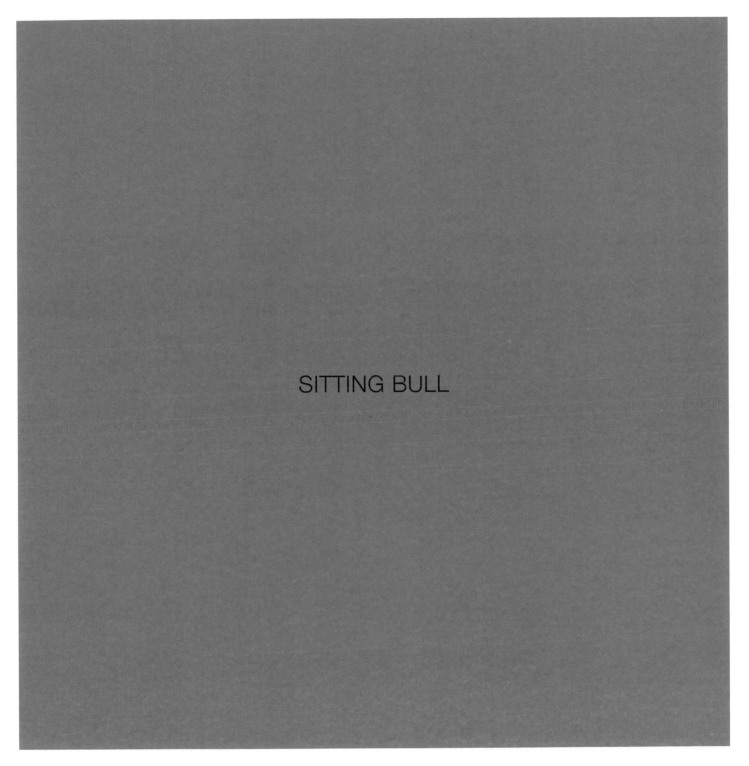

SITTING BULL

PANTS ...

OR SKIRT ?

"I don't meet competition. I crush it."

–Charles Revson

"Everything being a constant carnival, there is no carnival."

–Victor Hugo

61

YOUNG REBELS

DREADLOCKS

THE EXPLOSION

"IF YOU CAN'T IMITATE HIM, DON'T COPY HIM."

–Yogi Berra

"You have to do your own growing no matter how tall your grandfather was."

–Abraham Lincoln

"Never measure the height
of a mountain,
until you have
reached the top…

Then you will see how low it was."   –Dag Hammarskjold

"The trouble with children is that they are not returnable." —Quentin Crisp

–Ingrid Bergman, *Casablanca*

"Kiss me. Kiss me as if it were the last time."

LOVE AT FIRST SIGHT

"Teachers teach more by what they are than by what they say."

–Anonymous

"If your sibling gets something you want, you (1) try to take it; (2) break it; or (3) say it's no good."

—Patricia Fleming

VOILÀ

ONE-WAY
ALTERNATING ROAD

"A crown is merely a hat that lets the rain in."

"Though your enemy
is the size of an ant,
regard him
as an elephant."

–Danish Proverb

–Mark Twain

"My mother had a great deal of trouble with me, but I think she enjoyed it."

"If evolution really works, how come mothers only have two hands?"

—Milton Berle

ID PHOTO

"Do we need distance to get close?"

—Sarah Jessica Parker

FORTUNE COMING IN

"As the old cock crows the young cock learns."

–Irish Proverb

"I've seen things you people
wouldn't believe."

—Blade Runner

STALKING

LAUREL
AND
HARDY

111

CONVERGENCE OF IDEAS

„We are like dwarfs standing upon the shoulders of giants."

–Bernard of Chartres

BABY ON BOARD

"Better a blonde today than a chicken tomorrow."

—A Beautiful Mind

"I don't know what my path is yet. I'm just walking on it." —Olivia Newton-John

"It's hard to be funny when you have to be clean." —Mae West

" Do not compute the totality of your poultry population until all the manifestations of incubation have been entirely completed."

–William Jennings Bryan

List of Breeds

Photo credits

✳ Peter Anderson/ Dorling Kindersley/Getty Images : page 51 ✳ Arco Digital Images/Tips Images : page 70 ✳ Bios/Tips Images : page 20, 29, 40, 41 ✳ Jane Burton/Warren Photographic : pages 4-5, 76-77, 96-97, 110, 124-125 ✳ John Daniels/ardea.com : pages 112, 113 ✳ Diamond Sky Images/Getty Images : pages 72, 75 ✳ Dorling Kindersley/Getty Images : page 50 ✳ Freudenthal Verhagen/Getty Images : pages 120-121 ✳ Russell Glenister/Corbis : pages 24-25, 39, 81 ✳ Ron Kimball/KimballStock . page 5 right, 11, 25 ✳ Jean Michel Labat/ardea.com : pages 1, 9, 16, 17, 18, 19, 32, 36, 37, 42, 43, 48, 52, 53, 56, 57, 60, 61, 79, 80, 88, 89, 99 bottom left, 99 bottom right, 119, ✳ Labat J.-M. & Roquette F./Bios/Tips Images : page 3, 114, 116-117 ✳ Lifeonwhite.com : pages 6, 7, 8, 13, 14-15, 26, 27, 30, 34, 35, 49, 54, 58 bottom, 58-59, 62, 63, 64, 65, 68-69, 84, 85, 86, 87, 90-91, 92, 93 bottom left, 93, 94, 95, 99 top left, 99 top right, 100,101, 102, 103, 104, 105, 106-107, 107 bottom 108, 109, 122, 123, 128, front cover ✳ PIER/Getty Images : pages 44-45 ✳ Tim Ridley/Getty Images : pages 82-83 ✳ Joel Sartore/Getty Images : pages 66-67, back cover ✳ Mark Taylor/Warren Photographic : pages 30-31, 111 ✳ Wave/Corbis : pages 23, 24 left, 47

METRO BOOKS
New York

An Imprint of Sterling Publishing
387 Park Avenue South
New York, NY 10016

METRO BOOKS and the distinctive Metro Books logo are trademarks of
Sterling Publishing Co., Inc.

© 2011 by Edizioni White Star s.r.l.

This 2011 edition published by Metro Books by arrangement with
Edizioni White Star s.r.l.

Translation: John Venerella
Editing: Suzanne Smither
Editorial Project: Valeria Manferto De Fabianis
Graphic Layout: Marinella Debernardi
Text: Giorgio Ferrero

ISBN 978-1-4351-3330-3

For information about custom editions, special sales, and premium and corporate purchases,
please contact Sterling Special Sales at 800-805-5489 or specialsales@sterlingpublishing.com.

Manufactured in China

1 3 5 7 9 10 8 6 4 2

www.sterlingpublishing.com